Children
OF THE BIBLE

Colleen L. Reece
and Julie Reece-DeMarco

BARBOUR
PUBLISHING

All scripture quotations are taken from the King James Version of the Bible.

Published by Barbour Publishing, Inc., P.O. Box 719, Uhrichsville, Ohio 44683, www.barbourbooks.com

Our mission is to publish and distribute inspirational products offering exceptional value and biblical encouragement to the masses.

Member of the
Evangelical Christian
Publishers Association

Printed in the United States of America.

Contents

For seven special children:

Alexa, Gabrielle, Sophia, Natalie, Cade, Ella, and Micah

from Colleen and Julie

Introduction

Children have always played a vital part in God's dealings with His people. Reading about them enriches our knowledge of long-ago life and customs.

Children of the Bible shares the disappointments, joys, and triumphs of children who step from between the pages of the Bible and into the twenty-first century. Their lives and stories help stimulate imagination and instill Christian principles—principles as applicable now as in days past. What better way to become grounded in the best of all possible literature than with stories from the world's best-selling, most important Book?

While *Children of the Bible* is not specifically geared toward children, they will find excitement in discovering biblical counterparts. The stories can be used as read-alouds, part of family devotions, discussion starters, or teaching examples of the rewards of right behavior.

Adults as well as children are reminded that the God who cared for His people thousands of years ago is the same Master, Savior, and Friend who cares for us today.

Note: Some of the "characters" used in Children of the Bible *are not named or referred to specifically, such as the lad with the loaves and fishes, the daughter of Jairus, etc. Although many characters, situations, and dialogue herein are products of the authors' imaginations, nothing contained in this book contradicts scripture in any way.*

Old Testament

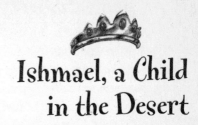

Ishmael, a Child in the Desert

Genesis 16, 21

Ishmael rubbed his eyes until tears came. They washed away some of the sand that had blown into them. Ishmael looked to the left, the right, in front of him, and behind him. There were no other people or towns as far as he could see. Just him, his mother, Hagar, and the very hot desert.

Ishmael's mouth felt dry. His head hurt. He wanted a drink badly. But the water was all gone from the bottle his mother carried. There were no rivers or wells. He and his mother were going to die—and it was all his fault.

"If only I hadn't made fun of my brother Isaac and his mother, Sarah, Father Abraham would never have sent Mother and me away," Ishmael whispered, so low Hagar could not hear him. It would make her feel bad to know he blamed himself.

"Creep under the bushes," Hagar told her son.

Ishmael obeyed, glad to be shaded from the burning sun.

Hagar went a little way off and began to cry. Ishmael cried, too. He buried his head in his hands, thinking thoughts too bitter to put into words. *God, it wasn't my mother's fault Sarah gave her to Abraham so he could have a son. She was only an Egyptian maid. She had no choice. She had to obey. It is true Mother despised Sarah when she knew she was going to bear a child, but how could Father Abraham let Sarah treat Mother so harshly she was forced to flee?*

Ishmael wiped the sweat and tears from his face, his heart burning with anger and disappointment. He thought about what had happened when Sarah drove his mother away. He had heard the story more times than he could count. On the way to Shur, Hagar had stopped by a fountain of water in the wilderness. Too bad there was no fountain now! Ishmael would give anything for a drink of water. Or for an angel of the Lord to appear, as one had that long-ago day.

"Where did you come from, and where will you go?" the angel had asked Hagar.

"I flee from Sarah," she'd replied.

The angel had told her to go back to Sarah, promising God would bless her with a multitude of children and grandchildren. The angel also had told her she carried a son whose name would be Ishmael, because the Lord had heard her affliction. Ishmael would be a wild man, whose hand would be against every man, with every

10

man's hand against him.

Through all the hard times, Ishmael had clung to the angel's words, glorying in the promise of what was to come.

Now he shook his head. *Where is the angel now?* his heart cried out. *Where is the God who made promises that will never come to pass? We will die here in this place and, with us, the promises.*

God heard Hagar and Ishmael crying. He felt sorry for them. One of His angels called to Hagar from heaven, saying, "Don't be afraid! God has heard Ishmael crying. Lift him up and take his hand. Someday your son will lead a great nation."

God opened Hagar's eyes. She saw a well of water in the desert where there had been none. She filled the bottle with water. "Ishmael! Come, we are delivered!" She and Ishmael drank and drank until they were filled.

God forgave Ishmael for his doubts and for tormenting Isaac and Sarah. He stayed with Ishmael while the boy grew up. Ishmael learned how to use a bow and arrows and live in the desert.

When Ishmael became a man, God made him the leader of a great nation, just as He had promised.

Isaac Trusts
His Father

Genesis 17–18, 22

Several years after Ishmael was born, God appeared to Abram. He told Abram he would have many children and be the father of many nations. He changed Abram's name to *Abraham*, which means "father of many," and Sarai's name to *Sarah*, calling her a "mother of nations."

Abraham laughed. He was one hundred years old. Sarah was ninety. How could they have children?

Then some days later, as Abraham was sitting in the tent door on the plains of Mamre, three men appeared during the heat of the day. Abraham offered them food and water. One of the strangers, affirming the word that God had already given, told Abraham he and Sarah would have a son.

Sarah, who was inside the tent, laughed at the stranger's idea. She, have a son at her age? *Impossible!*

With God, nothing is impossible. Isaac was

born, just as God had told Abraham and Sarah. He grew into a fine young lad.

Early one morning, Father saddled his donkey. "Come," he told his son Isaac and two servants. "God has called me to the mountain. We must take wood and fire for the burnt offering at the place God has told me."

A trip with Father? How exciting! Isaac's heart pounded, and he flew to get ready. Yet all through their journey, he wondered why Father looked so sad. He longed to ask, but something in his father's face kept him silent.

Three days after leaving their home, Abraham said to the servants, "Stay here with the donkey. My son and I will go worship and then come back here."

Isaac trotted up the trail, his shorter legs trying to keep up with his father's long steps. Father carried the fire and a knife. Isaac felt proud that his father let him carry the wood.

"Father," Isaac said.

"Here am I, my son."

Isaac felt puzzled. "Behold, the fire and the wood, but where is the lamb for the burnt offering?" he asked.

"My son, God will provide a lamb for the burnt offering," Father Abraham told him, and they both went on together.

When they reached the mountaintop to which God had directed them, Abraham built an altar where they could worship God as was their custom. He laid the wood on it. Then he tied Isaac up and put him on top of the wood.

"What is happening?" Isaac cried. He looked all around, but there was no lamb in sight. He looked back at his father, trying to understand. Where was the lamb God was supposed to provide for the burnt offering? Why had Father tied him up and placed him on the altar?

Abraham picked up the knife. For a moment, Isaac felt afraid. Then he remembered how much his father loved him. Even though everything was strange, Isaac trusted his father. His heart told him Father would never harm him.

Suddenly an angel called from heaven, telling Abraham not to harm Isaac. Then Abraham noticed a ram caught in the bushes by his horns. Abraham untied his son, caught the ram, and offered him as a burnt offering.

"We shall call this place *Jehovah-jireh*, which means 'in the mount of the Lord, it shall be seen,'" Abraham told Isaac.

The angel of the Lord called out of heaven a second time. He said because Abraham trusted his Father in heaven so much, God would bless him with so many children and grandchildren, they would be like stars in the sky! All the nations of the earth would be blessed because Abraham had obeyed God.

Abraham and Isaac went back to the servants and the donkey. It was time to go home.

Jacob and Esau, Twin Brothers

Genesis 25, 27, 33

Isaac was forty years old when he married Rebekah. Their hearts ached when they realized she could not have children. Yet Isaac did not give up hope. He himself was the child of Abraham and Sarah, who laughed when God told them they would bear a son in their old age. Surely God would hear his pleas for Rebekah to have a child.

God heard Isaac's prayers. He blessed Rebekah with twins!

When the children struggled inside Rebekah's body, she asked the Lord what was happening. He said she carried two nations in her body. He also told her one people would be stronger than the other and the older child would serve the younger. Rebekah thought this strange, as it was her people's custom that the oldest son was always favored.

In due time, Esau was born, hairy and red. Jacob followed—and his hand was holding Esau's heel.

As they grew, the boys were quite different. Esau loved the woods and became a cunning hunter. Jacob did not like hunting. He preferred farming and raising crops.

Isaac loved both of his sons but favored Esau. Isaac loved eating the venison (deer meat) his older son brought to him. Rebekah loved Jacob the most and wanted him to have the best of everything.

One day Esau came in from the fields. Jacob had a big pot of stew on the fire. "Feed me," Esau said. "I am so weary and hungry I feel faint."

Jacob saw the opportunity to get his brother's most highly valued possession—Esau's heritage as the oldest son, something Jacob had long envied and desired for himself. "I will give you my food if you will sell me your birthright," he told Esau.

For the firstborn male to sell his birthright was a serious thing and was rarely even considered, but Esau had a surprising response. "What good is a birthright when I am ready to die?" he demanded. "I swear it is yours if you give me food."

Jacob then fed his brother, very pleased he had Esau's heritage for just some bread and a bowl of lentil stew.

The birthright was not the only possession Jacob took from his brother. Years later when Isaac was old, his eyesight failed. He called Esau and asked him to bring venison so he might eat and then bless Esau, his firstborn, before he died.

Rebekah had listened to Isaac's conversation with his older son. She wanted Jacob, the younger, to receive the blessing instead of Esau. So, while Esau was out hunting for deer, she told Jacob to quickly bring two young goats and she would make meat for Isaac. She wrapped Jacob in goatskins, so Isaac would think he was Esau, the hairy one. Her trick worked. Jacob told his father he was Esau and received the special blessing his father had reserved for his older son.

When Esau learned what had happened, he wept bitterly. Not only had he sold his birthright for food, now Jacob had stolen the blessing that was rightfully his. "Father, have you no blessing for me?" Esau pleaded.

Isaac sadly said, "I have made Jacob your lord and all his relatives have I given to him for servants. What can I do for you, my son?"

"Bless me, also," Esau cried.

Isaac told Esau he would live by the sword, but one day, he would break free from serving his brother. Esau was so angry he determined to kill Jacob, but Rebekah sent her younger son away to protect him.

Years passed before the brothers met again. When they did, Jacob bowed to his brother seven times. Esau ran to meet Jacob and embraced him in forgiveness. At last, they were truly brothers, each blessed by God.

Joseph and His "Rainbow" Coat

Genesis 37

Jacob was also called Israel, because as a prince, he had power with both God and men. Jacob had many children, yet he loved his son Joseph the most. Joseph was born when Jacob was very old.

One day Jacob called Joseph to him. He said, "See, my son, I have made you a coat." He held out a garment very different than the usual clothing his sons wore. Jacob had obviously put a lot of effort into making it.

Joseph's eyes opened wide. Never in all his years had he seen such a coat. It had so many colors, it looked like a rainbow.

Joseph quickly put it on. "Thank you, my father," he said. "I will wear it proudly." He ran off to show his brothers his new coat.

Joseph's brothers were not happy at all. Why should their younger brother receive such a gift? Their father had never made any of *them* a coat of many colors, even though they helped feed the flock just as Joseph did. It made them so angry they wouldn't even speak a kind word to Joseph.

"Father Jacob always did love him best," they muttered among themselves. "He makes no attempt to hide it." The more they thought about it, the more they grew to hate their younger brother.

One night Joseph had a dream that made his brothers hate him even more. He dreamed his brothers were binding sheaves of grain in the field. "My sheaf rose and stood upright," he told them. "Your sheaves all stood roundabout and bowed down to my sheaf."

"You think you are going to reign over us?" his brothers demanded. "We shall see about that."

Before they could think what to do with him, Joseph had another dream that didn't increase his popularity. He told his brothers, then his father, "Behold, the sun and the moon and the eleven stars bowed down to the earth before me."

It made Joseph's brothers hate and envy him more than ever. Even worse, their father rebuked him. "What is this tale you tell? Young as you are, do you think you are going to rule over us all?"

Joseph didn't know what to say. He only knew what happened in his dreams.

One day, Joseph's brothers went out to feed the flock of sheep in Shechem. Jacob called Joseph to him. "Your brothers are feeding the flock in Shechem beyond the vale of Hebron. I want you to go to them and see how they fare, then return to me with word of them."

"Yes, Father. I will go find out if everything is going well." He proudly put on his coat of many colors and set out to find his brothers. As he was wandering in the field, he came across a man.

"What do you seek?" the stranger asked.

"I am looking for my brothers. Tell me, I pray, where they feed their flocks."

"They have already left this area," the man said. "I heard them say they were going to Dothan."

So Joseph continued his journey and went to Dothan.

When they saw him coming in his "rainbow" coat, Joseph's brothers grew more and more angry. "We will not bow down to him," one said. "Instead, we will kill him and throw him in a pit. We will tell Father Jacob a wild animal ate him!"

Reuben Saves His Brother

Genesis 37

The suggestion to kill Joseph, put him in a pit, and say an evil beast had eaten him found favor among most of the brothers. "Here comes the dreamer," they said to each other when they spotted Joseph's colorful coat a long distance away. "We shall see what becomes of our younger brother's dreams of us becoming his servants. That young boy will not rule over *us*."

Joseph's brother Reuben refused to kill Joseph. "Shed no blood," he told the others. "Just leave him in the pit." He didn't tell them he meant to sneak back, free Joseph, and return him to their father.

Joseph had no idea how much his brothers hated him or what they meant to do. He was just there to find out if they were well, so he could go home and report to his father. "What are you doing?" Joseph cried when they seized him and tore his coat of many colors from his body. "Why are you treating me so?"

His protests didn't stop them. They threw

him into a pit that held no water and left him there. All Joseph's cries for help did no good. Soon only the dry, hot land heard his frantic pleas to be released.

Joseph's brothers sat down some distance away to eat bread, well pleased with having rid themselves of the boy who said they must bow down to him. Before long, a company of Ishmaelite traders came by, bound for Egypt. Their camels were loaded with spices, balm, and myrrh.

Judah, one of the brothers, had a bright idea. "Joseph is our brother," he said. "What good is it to kill him and have to cover up his blood? Let's sell him to this caravan. That way we won't have his blood on our hands. Besides, we'll make some money." The others—except Reuben, who had been away when the caravan came by—thought it a fine idea. Before Reuben could return to his brothers, they lifted Joseph from the pit and sold him to the Ishmaelites.

When Reuben returned and went to the pit, he softly called his brother's name. "Joseph?"

His only answer was silence, deep and frightening.

"Joseph?" Reuben called again, looking into the pit. It was empty! His brother was gone. Reuben tore his clothes and went back to his brothers. What could they tell Father Jacob?

The brothers decided they must cover up

what they had done. They killed a goat and put some of its blood on Joseph's beautiful coat of many colors. The brothers traveled the long miles back to their home and their father, who waited for a son who would not come. When they reached Jacob, they told him, "We found this. Tell us, please, is it the coat you made for Joseph?"

Jacob took the stained coat from them. He said, "It is my son's. A wild animal surely has torn Joseph to pieces." He wept bitterly for the son he thought was dead.

Joseph was not dead. God had helped Reuben stand up to his brothers and save Joseph's life. While Jacob mourned his lost son, Joseph had been sold to Potiphar, the captain of the guard for the Egyptian pharaoh.

Benjamin, the Youngest Child

Genesis 42–46

Benjamin watched his brothers ready themselves for the long journey that lay ahead of them. After seven years of bountiful harvests, trouble had spread over every country like a smothering woolen blanket. The food supply was already low, and who knew how many failed crops lay ahead? Something had to be done.

In the midst of their worry, good news came. It ran through the land of Canaan like a river in flood. "There is corn in Egypt. People from every country are hastening there to buy food."

Jacob called his sons together. "Why do you stand there looking at each other? There is corn in Egypt! Hurry down there and buy for us, so we may live."

Benjamin's heart pounded with excitement. *Egypt!* The mysterious country about which he had heard so much. He could hardly wait to see it.

"Benjamin, you will remain here with me," Jacob said.

Questioning Jacob's decision was not permitted, but the boy's desire to see Egypt was so great he could not control himself. "I must go with my brothers, Father!" he burst out.

A lightning flash of anger came into Jacob's face. "Hold your tongue! I have said you shall stay."

"Yes, Father." Benjamin dug his toe in the dusty ground. It was hard being the youngest son. It seemed his father never let him do any of the things his brothers did. "Just because a wild beast killed Joseph doesn't mean I'm going to get hurt," he said, too low to be heard. "That was a long time ago. Besides, what could happen, with ten strong brothers to take care of me?"

For one wild moment, Benjamin considered sneaking away, keeping enough distance between him and his brothers that he would remain undiscovered until they were too far away to turn back. The corners of his mouth turned down. *No.* He wouldn't. He had already angered his father today by questioning his wishes. Instead he asked, "Why does Egypt have food when we don't?"

Some of Jacob's anger died. "I do not know, my son."

What Jacob didn't know was that God had spoken to Joseph, now second in command over all of Egypt. Seven years earlier, the pharaoh had dreamed about kine (or cattle) and corn. No one could tell him what his dream meant. God told Joseph it meant there would be seven years of plenty, followed by seven years of famine. Pharaoh listened to Joseph, made him governor over the land, and had him store food during the good harvests.

Only nine of Benjamin's brothers came back home with food. Simeon had been arrested. Joseph—the governor of Egypt whom none of his brothers had recognized—sent word that Benjamin must come to Egypt to prove the brothers were not spies!

Jacob refused to consent until the food they had brought home from Egypt was almost gone. He wept when he told his excited son good-bye.

Benjamin and his brothers got food in Egypt, but on the way home, Joseph's steward, who had followed the men, found a silver cup in Benjamin's sack of grain. When the steward took them back to the governor's house, the governor said the boy must stay in Egypt and be his slave!

"Father Jacob will die if Benjamin does not come home," his brothers protested.

The governor was so glad to hear his father was alive that he told the men who he really was. "I am your brother Joseph, and I have forgiven you," he said. "I believe God allowed me to be sold so that all these years later, the family wouldn't starve. Here are fine clothes for you."

He turned to Benjamin who stood staring. "Here are three hundred pieces of silver for you."

Benjamin was speechless. His eyes shone as brightly as the coins! And when Jacob and his family moved to Egypt, Benjamin rode on top of a wagon and was the happiest of all!

Moses Goes for a Boat Ride

Exodus 1–2

Joseph and his brothers had many children. Those children had even more children, so many that the Hebrews, called "the children of Israel," outnumbered the Egyptians. They became so powerful and were so fruitful that they filled the land.

One day a new pharaoh became ruler of Egypt. He feared losing his high position. He called his supporters together and said, "The children of Israel have multiplied until they outnumber us. This is a bad thing and must be stopped—now! Every day they become more of a threat to our nation. If war should come, they will surely rise up, join our enemies, and fight against us." He scowled. "There is only one thing to do. We will make their lives miserable. I will set taskmasters over these Hebrews and so afflict them that they will no longer be a threat."

Pharaoh did what he promised. He forced the children of Israel to build treasure cities— Pithom and Raamses. Yet no matter how greatly burdened the people were, they refused to allow Pharaoh to drive them away. The more they were persecuted, the more they multiplied and grew.

This angered Pharaoh so much that he gave a terrible order to the Hebrew midwives, Shiphrah and Puah. "When you help the Hebrew women deliver their babies, you must permit the girl babies to live, but you must kill all the boy babies!"

Shiphrah and Puah feared God. They refused to do what Pharaoh said, and they saved the boy babies.

When Pharoah called for the midwives, asking them why they let the boy babies live, they told him, "The Hebrew women are stronger than the Egyptian women. They deliver their own babies before we are called."

The pharaoh's rage burned like fire. "Every Hebrew boy who is born must be thrown into the river!" he declared.

About that time, a man of the house of Levi married a daughter of Levi. The woman conceived, and when her son was born, he was a goodly child. Even though she and her husband knew the pharaoh had ordered their little boy must be thrown into the river, they refused to obey. It might mean their own death as punishment, but they would not kill their child.

For three fearful months, the child's mother kept the baby hidden, never knowing when someone might betray her. The king's servants might burst into her humble home at any moment and tear her baby from her arms. At last she knew it was no longer safe to keep him at home. "Lord God of Israel, what can I do?" she whispered in agony. "I cannot, I will not, throw my child into the river!"

The river. That was it. She would make a small ark of reeds and put the baby inside. Then she would pray for her Father in heaven to protect her child, as she no longer could.

With loving hands and eyes blinded by the sea of tears that fell when she set to her task, the woman carefully covered a basket with tar and pitch. No water must be allowed to seep inside. She put the child in the basket and hid it in the bushes beside the river. It was the only way she could save her baby's life. She looked down at her empty arms and prayed her baby would be safe in the arms of the river and her God.

Miriam, a Caring Sister

Exodus 2

Miriam watched her mother put the basket holding her little brother into the water among the reeds. It looked like a little boat. What if it slipped into the current and sailed away? The Nile River was big; the ark was small. Would her brother cry when he found himself deserted? Would he be any safer than in their own home? What if a wild animal came by and discovered the helpless child lying in the ark?

Miriam felt sadder and more afraid than she had ever felt in her entire life. She could not bear to leave her little brother alone and unprotected. "I will stay and watch him, Mother," she quickly said. "I will watch carefully and come tell you what happens."

Her mother nodded and turned away, too filled with grief to speak.

Miriam found a hiding place far enough away that she could see but not be seen by anyone who might come along. She waited and waited. Nothing happened for a long time, except for the rustling of bushes that sent her heart leaping to her throat. When she saw it was only a bird, she relaxed.

Suddenly she heard voices. Her heart beat so loudly it made her chest hurt. What would happen to her if she were discovered? More important, what would happen to her brother if *he* were discovered?

Miriam held her breath and peered at the group of maidens who had come to wash themselves at the river. Her mouth flew open. She quickly put one hand over it to stifle a cry. It was the pharaoh's daughter and her friends— headed straight for the ark among the reeds! A few steps more and they couldn't help seeing the baby concealed in the basket that was gently rocking with the wash of the water.

"What is that?" the pharaoh's daughter exclaimed. "An ark?" She beckoned to a maid. "Bring it to me."

Miriam felt faint. Would Pharaoh's daughter take the little boy to her father, who would surely have him killed? In spite of her fear, Miriam crept closer. She heard her baby brother crying when the basket was opened. She clenched her small hands into fists and held them over her mouth so she would not cry out, also.

Pharaoh's daughter lifted the baby from the ark. "What are you doing here, little baby?" She looked closer. "Why, you are a Hebrew child!"

She cuddled the baby close in her arms.

Miriam could see the woman meant the child no harm. She stepped from the bushes and asked, "Shall I bring a Hebrew woman to you, to nurse the baby?"

"Yes, child. Go," Pharaoh's daughter told her.

Miriam ran home as quickly as she could. She burst into the house, where her mother was weeping. "Come, Mother!" Miriam shouted. "Pharaoh's daughter found my brother. She is kind. She will not let him be killed." She took a deep breath. "Mother, you are to be his nurse!"

"May the Lord God be praised!" her mother cried. She hurried with Miriam to the river, still weeping—this time for joy.

Pharaoh's daughter put the baby in his mother's arms. "Take him and care for him. I will pay you."

Miriam was so happy she danced all the way home!

When the child grew older, his mother took him to the pharaoh's daughter. The Egyptian woman claimed him as her son and called him *Moses*, which means, "saved from the water."

Samuel Hears God's Voice

1 Samuel 1–3

A certain woman named Hannah loved her husband, Elkanah, dearly. Her greatest desire was to give him a son. Yet as each new year followed, no child came to them. Hannah fell into despair. When she went to the house of the Lord, she wept and would not eat because she was childless.

Hannah grew desperate. She prayed to the Lord and vowed, *Lord, if You grant me a son, I will give him back to You for all the days of his life.* Although the words were only spoken in her heart, her lips moved.

Eli, a priest of the Lord who was watching Hannah pray, thought she was drunk. He told her to put away her wine!

Hannah quickly denied having had wine to drink. She told him she had been praying out of her anguish and grief.

Eli believed her. He said, "Go in peace. May the God of Israel grant your petition."

When the right amount of time had passed,

Hannah delivered a son. She named him *Samuel* (which means "heard by God"), saying, "Because I asked the Lord for him."

Hannah kept Samuel with her until he was old enough; then she took him to Eli. He was to serve with Eli, as she had promised the Lord. The child grew and was in favor with both God and man. He helped care for Eli, whose eyes had grown dim.

One night, a voice, clear and compelling, awakened the young boy. "Samuel. Samuel."

Samuel sat up and rubbed sleep from his eyes. He looked all around him. The voice didn't sound like Eli's, but what would anyone else be doing in the bedchamber at that time of night? "Who is there?" he demanded. "What are you doing in my room, and why are you calling me?"

There was no answer.

Samuel felt frightened. He ran to Eli, keeper of the temple, who lay sleeping not far away. He shook Eli's shoulder and said, "Here I am. Why did you call me?"

"I did not call you," Eli said. "Go back to bed."

Samuel couldn't understand what was happening. Someone had called him, but who? Only he and Eli were there, and Eli would never tell a lie. Had it only been a dream?

He slowly went back to his bed and lay down. "Samuel." The call was low but unmistakable.

This time Samuel knew he was not dreaming. He had to be asleep to dream, and he was not asleep! Again he ran to Eli. Again he said, "Here I am. Why did you call me?"

The old man said, "I did not call you, my son. Go back and lie down again."

Samuel was more frightened than ever. "I must be hearing things," Samuel said to himself, but he did as Eli said, then pulled his covers over his head and shivered.

"Samuel," came the voice again.

This time when the boy went to Eli, the old priest knew it must be God speaking to Samuel. Eli told the boy he had learned to love as his own, "If He calls again, say, 'Speak, for Your servant hears.'"

God? Speaking to me? What will happen next? Samuel wondered.

When the Lord came and stood beside the boy and called as He had before, Samuel followed Eli's directions and said, "Speak, for Your servant hears."

God told the young boy many things that would happen. They all did. God was with Samuel all the time he was growing up. When Samuel became a man, everyone knew the boy who had heard God's voice was a true prophet of the Lord.

David and His Sheep

1 Samuel 16–17

*C*ome here, little lamb!" David, the shepherd boy, called while hurrying after a lamb that had strayed from the flock David was keeping in his father Jesse's fields near Bethlehem. "Don't you know better than to leave your mother and go off by yourself?"

The naughty lamb, who wanted to run and play, didn't stop even long enough to look back at her keeper. *"Baa,"* she said, and ran faster than ever.

David groaned. He had been taught since childhood that when lambs and sheep separated themselves from the flock, they were in great danger. Wild animals lurked outside herds of sheep. If a bear or lion saw the little lamb all alone, she could well become his dinner.

"Come back, I say!" David ordered. The lamb didn't stop. David looked at the other sheep. All except the lamb were peacefully eating grass. David sighed. He hated leaving them but had no choice. Father Jesse had set him tending sheep because he trusted his son to care for them. Now, even though it meant leaving the body of the flock unprotected, he must go find and restore the wayward lamb to the fold. With an anxious glance at the large flock of animals, he set off to capture the frolicking lamb.

Before he got far, a plaintive *"Baa. Baa!"* sent David racing in the direction from which the cries were coming. His heart pounded. This *baa* was *not* the sound of a lamb leaping for joy. It was the sound of a lamb in danger, frantically crying out for help—a cry David had heard many times.

David soon discovered why the terrified lamb was bleating. A lion had grabbed her in his mouth and was carrying her off!

"Stop!" David shouted at the top of his voice.

The lion looked back at the boy but didn't release the lamb. He just continued on his way, still holding the bleating lamb in his mouth.

David lifted the rod (a stout club) he always carried to protect his flock from danger. "Please, God, help me save the lamb," he prayed. Strengthened by his prayer, and by days and nights of herding his flock in all kinds of weather, David brought his rod down with all his might. It struck the lion a terrible blow.

The lion opened his mouth to roar his rage. David grabbed the lamb out of his jaws. The lion turned on David, but the shepherd boy grabbed the lion's long hair. He hit him with the rod until the lion fell down dead.

David took the lamb in his arms. She was so scared she shook all over. David carried her back to the flock and set her by her mother. *"Baa!"* she cried. David laughed. That frightened little lamb wouldn't be leaving her mother and running away again for a long, long time.

Lions weren't the only thing David, keeper of the flocks, had to fear on behalf of his charges. Now and then a bear would come looking for an easy meal. Lambs were the best targets, because of their small size and inability to defend themselves. David was able to rescue a lamb from a bear in the same way he had saved the lamb caught in the lion's mouth. He prayed to God for help, then took up his rod and struck the bear with it until the lamb was saved.

David, His Harp, and Jonathan

1 Samuel 8–9, 16, 18

Samuel, the boy who heard God's voice and became a prophet, lived to be a very old man. His sons became judges over Israel, but they did not walk in the ways of the Lord. They took bribes and perverted judgment.

The people rose up in protest. They demanded that Samuel give them a king to rule over them, as other nations had.

Samuel was displeased. When he prayed, the Lord told Samuel, "The people have not rejected you, but Me, that I should not reign over them. Tell them what manner of king will rule them."

Samuel did as directed. He warned the people of the consequences of their demands, but they refused to obey his warning, saying, "We will have a king over us, who will judge us and go out before us and fight our battles."

God told Samuel to give them what they desired. God chose Saul, of whom it was said there was not a goodlier person among the children of Israel. Saul was powerful, and a head taller than any of the people. Samuel anointed Saul and set him apart as king.

Saul became a mighty leader, but after a time, he sinned and broke the commandments because he feared the people and obeyed them, rather than God. Samuel rebuked Saul and warned him the Lord had rejected him from being king.

One day God said to Samuel, "Go to Bethlehem. There you will find the king I have chosen, among the sons of Jesse."

Even though Samuel knew Saul would kill him if he discovered where he was going and why, Samuel obeyed. He reached Bethlehem and went to the home of Jesse. "Bring me your sons," he commanded.

First to come was Eliab. Surely this was the man the Lord had chosen to one day replace Saul. But God said, "Look not on the countenance or the height of his stature. The Lord does not see as man sees. Man looks on the outward appearance, but the Lord looks on the heart."

One by one, seven of Jesse's sons stepped forward. God did not choose any of them to be the new king.

"Have you more sons?" Samuel asked.

"Only David, my youngest. He is in the fields, caring for the sheep," Jesse said.

"Send for him," Samuel ordered.

David didn't know what to think when his

father sent word for him to leave the sheep and come to the house. He didn't think he had done anything wrong. Why, then, would Father Jesse send for him?

When David came to Samuel, God told the old prophet that David was the one. Samuel put oil on David's head and said a prayer. David would be king of Israel when he grew up.

God's Spirit came into the boy's heart. He had never felt so happy or excited.

David could play the harp, as well as take care of the sheep. One day the servants of King Saul came for David. "Our master has times of great trouble. Come play the harp for him, so he can find peace."

Saul liked David so much that he kept him at the palace part of the time. Whenever Saul felt sick, David played his harp. It always made Saul feel better.

When David came to the king's palace, he met Jonathan, Saul's son. They immediately became such strong friends that when Jonathan learned his father had grown jealous of David and planned to kill him, he warned his friend and saved his life.

David Meets
a Giant

1 Samuel 17

King Saul was at his wit's end. He paced the floor of his palace, shaking his head and roaring demands for his counselors to advise him. The Philistines, longtime enemies of God's people, were preparing to attack Saul's armies. They stood on a mountain on one side of a valley, while the Israelites stood on a mountain across from them. Worse, every day for forty days, the biggest, meanest of their rank taunted Saul's army, calling for someone to come fight him.

"Send me a man, any man!" he bellowed. "If he is able to fight me and win, we will be your servants. If I slay him, you will serve us. I defy the armies of Israel this day. Give me a man to fight."

"You have many brave men in your army," Saul's counselors reminded their king. "Three of them are the brothers of David, the shepherd boy. Your men are loyal, as well. Yet tell us, mighty king, how can any man fight Goliath? He is over nine feet tall, and he has brothers almost as tall as he!"

King Saul was sorely grieved, but he had no answer.

One day Jesse told his youngest son, "Take this grain and these loaves of bread to your brothers in the camp of Saul. Give these cheeses to their leaders and bring me word of my sons."

David rose early in the morning, left his sheep with a keeper, and headed for the battlefield. He reached the Israelite army just as they were preparing themselves to fight against the Philistines. David left his food with the man in charge of provisions and ran into the battle lines to find his brothers.

Suddenly Goliath rose to his full height, towering above lesser men. He wore full armor that covered him from head to toe, except for his sneering face. "Send someone to fight me!" he bawled. His loud, frightening voice scared King Saul's men. They turned and ran away!

David did not run away. "I will fight the giant," he said.

King Saul could scarcely believe his ears. "What did you say?" He shook his head in disbelief. "You, a mere boy? What foolishness is this?"

David refused to be intimidated by the king. "I have killed a lion and a bear that attacked my sheep," he said. "The God who saved me from the wild animals will save me now."

44

David's oldest brother, Eliab, was furious. "What are you doing here, anyway? Who is taking care of the sheep in the wilderness? I know how proud you are and how rebellious. You have come to see the battle."

The argument raged until at last King Saul agreed to let David fight. He dressed the boy in his own armor, but David laid it aside.

When Goliath saw David, the giant was enraged. He, fight a boy?

David cried, "I fight you in the name of the Lord! All the world will know there is a God in Israel. The battle is the Lord's. This day He will give you all into our hands." David took a stone from his bag. He put it in his slingshot and let it fly. *Wham!* It hit the wicked giant and killed him.

Goliath crashed to the earth so hard the ground shook. His unexpected defeat frightened the enemies, and they ran away. God had helped the shepherd boy who would one day be king of all Israel to save His people—just as He had helped David save the little lambs from the lion and the bear.

Solomon's Solution

1 Kings 2–3

David reigned over Israel for forty years: seven in Hebron and thirty-three in Jerusalem. He experienced defeat and victory, sorrow and joy. When he turned away from God and followed his own sinful desires, troubles poured down on him, but when he fell on his knees and repented, God forgave him.

God also blessed David with a special son named *Solomon*, which means "peaceable." When King David grew old, he proclaimed Solomon would be king over all Israel. He blessed Solomon and laid on him the responsibility of ruling the people. "Be strong, my son," David charged. "Show yourself a man. Do all the Lord requires. Walk in His ways. Keep His statutes and His commandments, His judgments and His testimonies that are written in the Law of Moses. If you do this, you will prosper in everything you do. Your kingdom will be far greater than my own."

Soon after, David died. Solomon ascended

to the throne. He loved the Lord and showed his love by living in accordance with his father's teachings.

One night in Gibeon, the Lord came to Solomon in a dream. "Ask what I shall give you."

Solomon replied, "You have shown my father David mercy as he walked before You in truth and righteousness. You gave him a son to sit on the throne. Lord, You have made me king instead of David." He sighed. "I am but a little child. I don't even know how to go out or come in. I am among the people You have chosen, so many they cannot be counted." He paused, then said, "I ask You to give me an understanding heart, so I may judge wisely and separate good from bad—for who can judge such a great many of Your people?"

God was pleased Solomon had humbly confessed his inadequacy and asked for help, instead of seeking something for himself. He said, "Because you asked for understanding and have not sought long life, or great riches, or for the death of your enemies, I will do according to your wishes. I have given you a wise and understanding heart. None who came before you, or who shall rise after you, shall be like you. I will also give you what you did *not* seek: riches and honor. If you will follow Me, as your father David did, I will lengthen your days."

Solomon awoke, knowing God would surely

give him the wisdom to judge.

His wisdom was tested a short time later. Two women came before him. Both claimed to be the mother of the same child. They had delivered their babies just three days apart, in the same house. On that third night, one of the babies died. When they came before King Solomon, one of the women cried, "When this woman discovered her child was dead, she laid him in my arms and stole my living baby!"

The other screamed, "It is not so! The child is mine."

Back and forth they argued, while Solomon pondered what to do. At last he said, "Bring a sword. Divide the baby into two parts and give one to each of the women."

A river of tears flowed down the real mother's face. "Don't kill my baby, my lord!" she pleaded. "Give him to her."

"Let him be neither hers nor mine," the other woman said. "Divide him."

"Do not kill the baby!" Solomon thundered. "Give him to the first woman. She is his mother."

All Israel heard of Solomon's judgment and feared the king. They saw the wisdom of God was within him to bring justice.

A Hungry Little Boy

1 Kings 17

All through history, God has cared for those who love and serve Him. Many times, such as when He sent quails and manna to the children of Israel, the Lord chose to provide help in miraculous ways. So it was with the prophet Elijah.

Wicked King Ahab (who did more evil in the eyes of the Lord than any who had gone before him—and they had certainly done enough) set up an altar and built a temple to worship false gods. He provoked God and angered Him more than all the previous kings of Israel.

Elijah warned Ahab there would be no rain or dew in the land for the next few years, except at his word. Because he dared speak so, he was no longer safe from the king and his men. God told His servant Elijah to hide by the brook Cherith, near the Jordan, and drink from it. He also commanded ravens to bring food to Elijah each morning and night.

After a time, the brook dried up for lack of

rain. God then told Elijah to go to Zarephath. He gave him detailed instructions about what to say to the widow he would meet at the gate of the city.

On the day Elijah reached Zarephath, a certain little boy watched his mother take a bit of flour from the barrel in which it was kept. He watched her pour a few drops of oil on it and make the tiniest cake imaginable.

The little boy was hungry—so hungry his stomach growled loudly. "It is hard to wait for the cake to be ready," he told his mother.

She shook her head and went on with her work. "I am sorry, son. The cake is not for us."

The boy's stomach growled again. He could not believe what his ears were hearing. "Not for us? Why not, Mother?"

"I met a man named Elijah when I went to get sticks for the fire," she said. "He asked me for a drink of water. I gave it to him. Then he asked me for a piece of bread."

"We have no bread!" the little boy burst out. "And this is the last of our flour and oil. How can we give the little cake to the stranger?" He crossed his arms over his empty stomach.

His mother's hands stilled. "I told the man that we had only a handful of provisions left. But he said if I would bring him a cake, we would always have flour and oil."

The boy peeked into the jars. "I don't see any. Mother, if you give our food away, we will both die."

"Something about Elijah made me trust him," the woman told her son. "I will take him the cake."

The little boy sadly watched her go. Not knowing why he bothered, he peeked into the jars again. He rubbed his eyes and looked once more. How could he have missed it? There was enough flour and oil for another cake!

Elijah stayed with the little boy and his mother. They always had enough flour and oil to make cakes.

One day the little boy got so sick he stopped breathing. Elijah prayed for him. God heard and answered Elijah's prayer. He healed the little boy. The woman and her son knew Elijah was truly a man of God. Both rejoiced because they had given him the little cake.

Elisha Helps
the Children

2 Kings 2, 4

God called many prophets to warn the people
to repent. In his old age, Elijah was told
by God to set Elisha apart as a prophet. One
day when they stood beside the river Jordan,
with fifty sons of the prophets observing from a
distance, Elijah rolled up his cloak and struck the
water. The river parted, allowing the men to cross
over on dry land.

Once on the other side, Elijah said, "I will
soon be taken away from you. What shall I do for
you before I go?"

Elisha replied, "Give me a double portion of
your spirit, that it may be upon me."

Elijah said, "You have asked a hard thing, but
if you see me when I am taken from you, it will
be yours. If not, it will be denied."

While they walked and talked, God sent
a chariot of fire and horses of fire. Elijah was
carried up to heaven in a whirlwind!

Elisha saw what happened. He cried, "My
father! My father! The chariot and horsemen of

Israel!" He tore his clothes apart, knowing he would see Elijah no more. Then he picked up the cloak Elijah had dropped. He struck the water. Again it parted, and he safely crossed over.

The watching prophets knew the spirit of Elijah was resting on Elisha.

Some time afterward, a certain woman came to Elisha. "My husband, who was your servant, is dead," she cried. "You know he feared and honored the Lord. Now his creditor is demanding that my two sons become his slaves, in order to pay my husband's debt."

"What do you have in your house?" Elisha questioned.

"Nothing except a pot of oil."

"Go to your neighbors," the prophet told her. "Borrow all the empty jars they will give you. Then go inside your house and shut the door. Pour oil from your vessel into the empty ones."

The woman stared at him, then did as she was told. Her sons watched in awe as the oil from her one pot filled every vessel. "We are out of jars," one son said.

"We are out of oil, too," the other added.

Elisha told their mother, "Go sell the oil. Pay your debt. There will be enough money left for you and your sons to live on."

During his travels, Elisha came to Shunem. A

rich but childless woman invited him to stay for a meal. After that, whenever he reached the city, he ate with them. They even made a room where he could stay when he came.

Elisha was so grateful he asked the woman what he could do for her, but she had all she needed except a son, for her husband was old. To her amazement, Elisha told her she would bear a son in about a year. It came to pass, just as Elisha had said.

The child grew until one day he went into the field where his father was working with the reapers. A terrible pain shot through his head. "My head, my head!" he screamed.

Servants carried him to his mother, but the boy only lived until noon.

The woman laid him on Elisha's bed and set out on a donkey to find Elisha. When they returned to her home, Elisha went to the child, closed the door behind him, and prayed. He lay full length on the boy and put his mouth to the child's mouth. The boy's flesh warmed. Elisha repeated the process.

"Achoo! Achoo!" The boy sneezed five more times; then he opened his eyes, healed by the power of God through His servant Elisha.

A Wise Little Servant Girl

2 Kings 5

Long ago it was the custom for armies to bring back children from other countries. These children became servants in the homes of those who took them captive. Naaman, captain of the Syrian army, brought a little maid out of the land of Israel. She became his wife's servant.

Naaman was a mighty man, a valiant soldier, and highly favored by his master, the king. Yet all was not well with him.

One day the little serving maid discovered her mistress in distress. "Why are you crying?" she asked. Even though the girl missed her own people, Naaman and his wife had treated her well. It made her heart ache to see her mistress so disturbed.

The woman wiped away her tears, but she could not wipe away the sadness of heart that showed in her troubled face. A fresh burst of tears gushed. "My husband, Naaman, has leprosy," she finally managed to say. "No one can help him. He will surely die. What will I do?

How can I live without him?"

The little maid felt tears crowd behind her own eyes. What a terrible thing to happen to Naaman—and to his wife, who would be desolate without him. What could she do? She was only a serving girl. They had everything; she possessed nothing except—her heart leaped with joy. Did she not have faith in God, and something to offer? "There is a prophet of God in Samaria," she excitedly said. "His name is Elisha. If your husband will go to him, he can be cured of his leprosy."

"Impossible!" the distraught woman cried. "No one can remove leprosy once it strikes."

"God can, and Elisha speaks with God," her maid whispered.

Still doubting, but desperate enough to grasp at the wind itself, Naaman's wife told her husband what the maiden had said.

Naaman didn't know what to think. Should he take the servant girl's advice? He had never heard of anyone who could cure leprosy.

Neither had the king of Syria, but he told Naaman he must make every effort to find someone who could. He sent his captain to the king of Israel carrying a letter that read, *I have sent you my servant Naaman, that you may cure him of his leprosy*. Naaman also took with him much gold, silver, and fine clothing.

The king of Israel tore his clothes when he

read the letter. "Am I God, to cure leprosy?" he demanded. But when Elisha heard what happened, he sent word to the king that Naaman should come to him.

When Naaman reached Elisha's house, he waited for the prophet to come out. Elisha didn't come. Instead he sent to Naaman a messenger who said, "Go wash seven times in the river Jordan, and you will be well."

Naaman grew angry. He had expected Elisha to come out and call on God to heal him. If all he needed to do was wash in river water, he could go home and wash in his own rivers!

One of his servants said to Naaman, "Sir, if Elisha had asked you to do something great, you would have done it. Why not try what he told you?"

Naaman listened to his faithful servant. He dipped himself into the Jordan. One, two, three, four, five, six times. Each time the leprosy was still there. "I will dip once more, then go home to die," Naaman vowed.

The seventh time he came out of the water, his leprosy was gone! Naaman fell down and thanked God. Then he hurried home to tell his wife the wonderful news—and to thank the wise little servant girl who had sent him to Elisha.

Josiah, the Boy King

2 Kings 21–23

M any, many kings ruled over Israel. Some were good; others were not. Sometimes a new king would be set on the throne when he was quite young. Manasseh was only twelve when he began his fifty-five-year reign over Jerusalem. He followed the abominations of the heathen and built altars to strange gods, made graven images, and wrought much wickedness.

His son Amon was no better. Amon became king over Jerusalem when he was twenty-two and ruled for the next two years. He did not love or serve God. He followed the path of his father, Manasseh, and did all sorts of evil things. Worst of all, he turned from the Lord God of his ancestors and worshipped the idols his father worshipped, bowing down before them in defiance to the one true God.

The only good thing that came out of Amon's reign was his son Josiah. From the time Josiah was just a young boy, he loved and tried to please God, in spite of his father's terrible example.

He did what was right in the sight of the Lord and walked in all the ways King David had proclaimed, not turning aside to either the right or the left.

This was not easy for Josiah. His heart ached because of his father's sins. "It is wrong for Father to do this and not obey God," he often whispered to himself, making sure no one could hear him. "It isn't because Father doesn't know the law. Everyone knows the law." He sighed, thinking back on all he had been taught.

Many years before Josiah or Amon was born, God had given Moses rules for the people of Israel. The rules were written on flat rocks called tablets. One rule warned the people: The Lord God was the only God they should worship. They were not to make idols or bow down and serve them. Yet King Amon had many ugly idols in his house. Josiah hated them. When he was very small, he made faces and stuck out his tongue at them when he passed by. As he grew older he refused to look at them at all. If only Father would throw them all away and obey God!

One day some of Amon's servants rose up and killed the king. This made the people of the land so angry they killed all the servants who had conspired against Amon. They also insisted on crowning Josiah as their king!

"How can I rule the people?" Josiah said in

despair. "I am only eight years old!"

God knew Josiah loved Him and had always tried to do right. He was pleased, and He helped Josiah be a good king.

Josiah served God all the days of his life. The "boy king" ruled in Jerusalem for thirty-one years. He went to the house of the Lord, and all the men of Judah and all the inhabitants of Jerusalem went with him, including the priests and the prophets. Josiah read to them the Book of the Covenant, which had been found in the temple. Standing by a pillar, he made a covenant with the Lord to follow His teachings. All the people pledged to do the same.

"Bring the vessels and everything that has to do with Baal and all the other false gods out of the temple of the Lord and from the grove," Josiah ordered. "They are to be burned outside Jerusalem in the fields of the Kidron Valley."

The priests did as commanded. The "boy king" had abolished idolatry.

Esther Saves Her People

Esther

*H*adassah, also called Esther, lost her parents when she was young. However, she was one of the more fortunate ones. Those without kinfolk who were orphaned were left with nowhere to go except the streets to beg for food and face the danger of being preyed on by wicked men. Esther escaped such a fate because of her uncle's son.

Mordecai was a Jew, as was Esther. He loved his cousin very much, so much that after her father and mother died, he took her into his home and raised her. He bestowed on her all the affection he would have given a natural-born daughter. Esther became a lovely girl, obedient and sweet-tempered.

About that time, a decree went out from King Ahasuerus, who reigned over 127 provinces, from India to Ethiopia. He appointed officers in all the provinces to gather every beautiful young maiden they could find, and bring them to the women's quarters of the palace in Shushan.

There they would be given all manner of beauty preparations by Hegai, the custodian of the women. In due time, King Ahasuerus would choose one of them to be his queen.

Esther was among the maidens to be taken to the palace. When Mordecai told her she was to go, she stared at him in disbelief. "We are Jewish. Surely the king will not want a Jewish queen!"

"He will not know you are Jewish," Mordecai told her. "You are beautiful enough to be queen. It may be God will one day use you to help our people."

Esther loved God. She loved her people. If she could help them, she would.

Before she left, Mordecai warned her again, "You must not tell anyone who your people or kindred are. No matter what happens, do not disclose this."

Esther did exactly as her cousin commanded.

Hegai was so pleased with Esther, she obtained his favor. He gave her seven choice maidservants from the king's palace. He moved Esther and her attendants to the finest place in the house of the women. Every day, Mordecai paced in front of the court of the women's quarters, so he could learn what was happening to her.

After twelve months of preparation, one by one, the girls appeared before Ahasuerus. None would go again, unless summoned by the king.

When he met Esther, he loved her more than all the others. He set the royal crown on her head and made her his queen. He made a great feast, the Feast of Esther, for all his officials and servants. He proclaimed a holiday and gave gifts.

Esther had not revealed she was Jewish to the king, but Mordecai kept in touch with her whenever he could. He warned her of a plot against her people, conjured up by the fiendish Haman, who wanted to occupy an even higher place than ruler of the princes. Haman hated Mordecai because Mordecai refused to obey the king's decree. He would not bow down to anyone except God. Haman told King Ahasuerus the Jewish people kept their own laws and not his. This angered the king, and he signed an order for all Jews to be killed.

Esther learned of the plot. She knew going to the king without being invited was dangerous. Yet she could not let the Jews be destroyed. She gathered her courage and bravely went to the king. She confessed she was Jewish and cleverly showed him Haman's wicked schemes. The king believed her. God had used Esther to save her people, just as Mordecai predicted.

Three Boys and a Terrible Fire

Daniel 3

King Nebuchadnezzar did not worship the God who created the heavens and the earth. He worshipped idols. He bowed down and sacrificed to them.

He charged the craftsmen in his employ to make an enormous image of gold. When it was finished, he ordered it set up in the province of Babylon. Then he called together all the important persons throughout the land to come to the dedication of the image that towered above the plain of Dura.

When the governors and counselors, treasurers and judges, and all the other officials of the provinces gathered and stood before the golden idol, a herald cried out, "To you it is commanded, all peoples, nations, and languages. Whenever you hear the sound of all kinds of musical instruments playing together in symphony, you shall fall down and worship the golden image King Nebuchadnezzar has set up. Any person who does not do so will immediately be cast into the midst of a burning, fiery furnace!"

Most of the people felt they had no choice except to obey. Each time they heard the music, they fell down to the ground and worshipped the ugly idol in order to save their lives, whether or not they felt it was right.

One day, some men came to Nebuchadnezzar. "O king, live forever," they chanted. Then they said, "You decreed that all should bow down and worship when the music sounds, lest they be cast into a fiery furnace." They shook their heads. "Even though you took Shadrach, Meshach, and Abednego into your palace and trained them, they ignore what you said. They do not hold you in high regard or serve your gods. All three of them refuse to bow down to the image of gold!"

King Nebuchadnezzar was furious. He sent for the three who had been accused. "Is it true?" he roared. "Either you will obey my commands and worship my idol, or you will be punished. I will have you thrown into a blazing furnace!"

Shadrach, Meshach, and Abednego had great faith in God. "The God we serve is able to save us from the hottest fire, if He chooses to do so," they told the king. "Even if He does not rescue us, we will not worship your gods or your golden image!"

The king almost choked with rage. He ordered the furnace to be heated seven times hotter than ever before. He had his guards bind and throw the three courageous friends into the fire. The flames were so hot that they killed those who thrust Shadrach, Meshach, and Abednego down into the depths of the fiery, burning furnace.

The king watched the fire rage. He rose in haste and demanded of his counselors, "Did we not cast three bound men into the fire?" He pointed with a shaking finger. "I see four men loose and walking in the midst of the fire. They are not hurt, and the form of the fourth man is like the Son of God. Bring them out!"

God honored the three children of Israel's great faith and delivered Shadrach, Meshach, and Abednego. Not a hair on their heads had been scorched. Not a single thread of their garments had been burned. Not one of them even smelled like smoke! King Nebuchadnezzar praised God for saving the brave friends who would not serve false gods, even if it meant losing their lives.

Daniel in the Lions' Den

Daniel 6

After the Lord delivered Daniel's friends from the fiery furnace, King Nebuchadnezzar was so impressed he made a new decree: "Any people, nation, or language which speaks against the God of Shadrach, Meshach, and Abednegeo shall be killed and their houses burned. There is no other God who can deliver like this!"

The king's change of heart should have ended Daniel's troubles, but it didn't. Many years later, Darius was crowned king. He placed 120 rulers over the kingdom, with three governors to watch them, so they wouldn't cheat him. Daniel was one of the governors. God's spirit was in Daniel, and he faithfully discharged his duties so well that King Darius began to consider making him ruler over the whole realm.

This infuriated the other rulers and governors. They were unable to find any fault in Daniel to report to the king, so they conceived a diabolical plot. "King Darius, we have consulted together to establish a royal law. Whoever petitions any god or man for thirty days, except you, shall be cast into the den of lions. Establish the decree and sign the writing so it cannot be changed," they pleaded.

King Darius, not suspecting their treachery, signed the decree.

"Did you hear what the king did?" a wild-eyed boy shouted to a group of companions near the palace. "He has thrown Daniel into the den of hungry lions!"

"Impossible!" his friends cried. "King Darius loves Daniel like a son. He would never do such a thing."

"He was tricked. His advisors talked him into signing a decree that whoever prayed to anyone but him for thirty days must face the lions." His face turned red with anger. "Daniel disobeyed. Three times every day he kneels down with his windows open toward Jerusalem and prays to God, just as he always has. I've seen him myself and so have you, only now it is against the law."

The smallest of the boys rubbed his eyes with a dust-grimed hand. "I don't want the lions to eat Daniel!"

"None of us do," another said, "but what can *we* do?"

"Nothing!" One boy spit out. "Once the law is signed and sealed by the king, it cannot be changed." He glanced around him to make sure no one could hear, then motioned for the other boys to huddle around him. "I wonder if the God Daniel prays to will save him. He saved the three children of Israel from the fiery furnace."

The boy who first brought the news whispered, "It is said that King Darius told Daniel, 'Your God whom you serve continually, He will deliver you.' " He ignored the ripple of surprise that swept through the little circle of boys. "We will know tomorrow. A stone has already been laid on the mouth of the lions' den. The king sealed it with his own signet ring, and with the signets of his lords. All we can do is wait—and pray."

The others looked at one another, nodded, and silently made their way home.

All that night King Darius spent fasting for Daniel. Early in the morning he went to the still-sealed lions' den. The most daring of the boys had slipped from their pallets even before the king arose and lay hidden outside the palace. Soon a great cry arose.

"Daniel lives! God sent His angel and shut the lions' mouths! Darius commands all men to tremble and fear before the God of Daniel, for He is the living God."

No one was happier that day than Darius and the boys who had witnessed God's power.

New Testament

A Baby Called John

Luke 1

Zacharias and his wife, Elisabeth, loved God more than anything in the world. They were righteous before Him and kept all His commandments.

One thing saddened their lives: They wanted a baby. Year after year came and went, until they both grew old. At last they realized they must live their lives childless. It was long past the time of life when Elisabeth could have a baby.

One day Zacharias was performing his service to God in the temple. A great crowd was praying outside. Zacharias glanced toward the right side of the altar and fell to his knees in fear. Was he seeing things? Surely the figure couldn't be an angel!

The angel spoke. "Don't be afraid, Zacharias. God has heard your prayer. You and your wife will have a baby boy. You shall call him John. He will be great in the sight of the Lord. He shall not drink wine or strong drink. He will be filled with the Holy Spirit even before he is born.

Many of the children of Israel will turn to God because of him."

Zacharias could only stare, but the angel wasn't finished speaking.

"He will go before God in the spirit and power of Elijah to turn the hearts of the fathers to the children, and the disobedient to the wisdom of the just, to make ready a people prepared for the Lord."

Zacharias shook his head. "How can I know this?" he brokenly inquired. "I am an old man, and my wife is well advanced in years. We are far too old to have a child."

The angel said, "I am Gabriel, who stands in the presence of God. I was sent by God to tell you these things and to bring you these glad tidings. You did not believe my words, which will be fulfilled in their own time. Behold, you will not be able to speak again until the day these things take place."

The people outside marveled that Zacharias stayed so long in the temple. When he came out and tried to speak, no words came out of his mouth! The people perceived he had seen a vision, for he beckoned to them but remained speechless.

For many, many months Zacharias could only silently go his way, even though his heart clamored for joy and he wanted to shout his gladness. Things had happened just as the angel

Gabriel said they would. Elisabeth was with child. She hid herself for five months, saying God had dealt with her in this way to take away the shame she felt when she could not have a child.

Time passed and still Zacharias could not speak. Then one glad day, Elisabeth delivered a healthy baby boy. Their joy was complete—and shared by their neighbors, who rejoiced that the Lord had shown such great mercy to Elisabeth and given her a child.

"What will you call him?" they asked. "Zacharias, after his father?"

Elisabeth shook her head. "His name will be John."

"There is no one among your relatives who is called by this name," they protested. Turning, they made signs to his father, asking him what the baby should be called.

Zacharias asked for a writing tablet. He wrote, *His name is John.* The people marveled. Immediately, Zachariah's speech returned, and he praised God.

John, later called John the Baptist because he baptized people in the river Jordan, grew up and did just as Gabriel had said. Many people believed in God because of John's preaching.

The Coming of God's Own Son

Matthew 1–2; Luke 1–2

A young maiden named Mary lived in the city of Nazareth, which was in Galilee. People from other towns looked down their noses at Nazareth and those who dwelled there. They often said nothing good could come out of Nazareth.

Those people were wrong. God chose Mary of Nazareth to be the mother of His own Son.

In the sixth month of the year God had chosen for His Son to come to earth, Mary was betrothed to a man named Joseph, a descendant of King David.

One day, the angel Gabriel, who had announced the birth of John to Zacharias, came to Mary. "Rejoice," the angel said. "You are highly favored of the Lord. He is with you. Blessed are you among women!"

Mary was troubled. Whatever could he mean?

Gabriel told her, "Do not be afraid, Mary. You have found favor with God. You will conceive and bring forth a Son and shall call His name *Jesus*. He will be great, and will be called the Son of the Highest. The Lord God will give Him the throne of David, and He shall reign over the house of Jacob forever. Of His kingdom, there will be no end."

"How can this be?" Mary asked. "I am not yet married."

Gabriel said, "The Holy Spirit will come upon you, that the Holy One who is to be born will be called the Son of God. Your cousin Elisabeth, although stricken with old age, is in her sixth month of carrying a child. With God, nothing is impossible."

Mary trusted God. She said to Gabriel, "Let it be to me according to your word."

After the angel departed, Mary rose and went into the hill country to see the wondrous thing that had happened to Elisabeth. She remained with Elisabeth for three months before returning home to wait for her own Son to be born.

Mary learned that Caesar Augustus had ordered everyone to report to the city in which they had been born, in order to be taxed. Mary and her husband, Joseph, traveled from Nazareth to Bethlehem, where Joseph had been born.

Mary was so tired from the long trip, she could barely keep going.

Joseph tried to find room for them at the inn, but the town was crowded with those who had also come a long way. Joseph knew they had to find shelter. It was time for Jesus to be born.

All Joseph could do was take Mary to a barn. When Jesus came, Mary wrapped him in warm clothing and put him in a manger. Jesus' first bed was a feed box for cattle.

Shepherds were in the field with their flocks that night. Suddenly an angel came. The shepherds were so frightened they fell down to the ground. The angel said, "Don't be afraid. Jesus, the Savior you have been waiting for all these years, is born. You will find Him in a manger." More angels came than the shepherds could count. They praised God and said, "Glory to God in the highest! On earth, peace and good will toward men."

After the angels left, the shepherds went to Bethlehem. They found Mary and Joseph, and little Jesus, just as the angels had said. The shepherds fell down and worshipped Him, then hurried away and told everyone they could find that Jesus had been born in Bethlehem.

Jesus Is
Blessed

Luke 2

Following the birth of Jesus, Mary and Joseph left Bethlehem. They traveled to Jerusalem so Jesus could be blessed in the temple when he was eight days old, as was the custom.

At the time Jesus was born, a certain man named Simeon lived in Jerusalem. He had loved and served God all the days of his life and was filled with the Holy Spirit. Simeon eagerly awaited the coming of the Promised One the prophets of old had foretold would someday come to deliver God's people from bondage. If only he, God's humble servant, could live to see that day, he would die in peace.

God was pleased with Simeon. He knew the desires of the devout man's heart. God promised Simeon he would not die until he had seen the Son of God.

Many years passed. Simeon's heart leaped within him when Mary and Joseph brought Jesus to the temple. He realized the promise God had made to him had come to pass. Simeon joyfully took Jesus up into his arms. He blessed God, crying, "Lord, now let Your servant depart in peace, according to Your word! I have seen Your salvation, which You prepared before the face of all people, a light to bring revelation to the Gentiles and the glory of Your people Israel."

Mary and Joseph marveled when Simeon spoke of their tiny Son. Then Simeon turned to them. He blessed them and said to Mary, "This Child is destined for the fall and rising of many in Israel, and for a sign which will be spoken against. Yea, a sword shall pierce through your own soul, also, that the thoughts of many hearts may be revealed."

At that very instant, they were interrupted by someone else who was in the temple that day. Anna was eighty-four years old. Her husband had died many years before, after he and Anna had only been married seven years. Anna served God in the temple, fasting and praying both day and night. She was a prophetess, one whom God had chosen to discern many things that would happen in the future.

When Mary and Joseph brought Jesus to the temple, Anna's heart pounded in her aged chest, like someone knocking on a door, demanding entrance. Just as Simeon had realized the truth minutes earlier, so Anna also knew through the Holy Spirit that Jesus was God's gift to the world. She knew God had sent Him so everyone who listened to His words and believed in Him could be saved from their sins and one day live in heaven with God and Jesus. She gave thanks to the Lord, and she spoke of Him to all those who looked for redemption in Jerusalem.

Jesus was just a baby. He was too young to know all these things—too young to know that for many, many years holy men of God had told of His coming; too young to know the prophet Isaiah had long ago said He would be called Wonderful, Counselor, the mighty God, the everlasting Father, the Prince of Peace. Yet all those things—and much more—happened after Jesus was blessed in the temple.

For now, Joseph and Mary pondered what Simeon and Anna had said. Then, having fulfilled the requirements of the Law of the Lord, they traveled back to their own city, Nazareth in Galilee.

Jesus Is Missing!

Luke 2

During the next few years Jesus grew to be strong and wise. Every year, His parents went to Jerusalem for what was called the Feast of the Passover. This observance reminded Jews how God had taken care of them long ago when they were in the land of Egypt.

What a time of joy and excitement! Families traveled caravan style, camping together along the way and making the most of the pilgrimage that became a holiday, especially for the younger members in the noisy group.

The year Jesus was twelve, He also went to Jerusalem for the holiday. Surely His boyish heart beat faster at the thought of being with the family and friends who thronged the roads on their way to Jerusalem! In the way of young boys ever since time began, the opportunity to see a world far different from His own must have heightened His senses to all that surrounded Him: dusty roads; the clamor of the multitude and the bray of donkeys; the sight and sound of

Roman soldiers on patrol, ordering the people to make way; the pungent odor of sweat and camel dung that assaulted His nostrils; the welcome taste of water from a goatskin bag.

When they reached their destination and looked into the city, Jerusalem in all its glory lay before them. Jerusalem, a city of unexplored wonders for those visiting it for the first time since being brought as tiny babies by their parents to be blessed. How different from Nazareth! The most awe-inspiring sight was the temple, the place all devout Jews believed to be the dwellingplace on earth of the most High God.

Those who came to Jerusalem always stayed for several days before turning their steps back to their homeland. They would cherish the memories of the Feast of the Passover until another year passed and the time to return to offer sacrifices and pay homage to their God came again.

After the holiday ended, the large group began the journey home. On the second day, Mary went to Joseph. She looked worried. "Do you know where Jesus is?" she asked.

"Perhaps He is among our kinfolk and acquaintances," Joseph said.

"I cannot find Him," Mary told him.

From family to family they went, searching for the missing boy. He was nowhere to be found.

Jesus must have been left behind in Jerusalem! His parents looked at one another in alarm. How would a twelve-year-old boy get along in the great city?

Mary and Joseph left the others and hurried back to Jerusalem. After three frightening days of looking for Jesus, they found Him in the temple. He was listening and talking with the wise men there. All those who heard were surprised such a young boy could know so much.

When Mary and Joseph saw and heard Him, they were amazed. Could this be Jesus, their Son, debating with those so much older and wiser than He?

After a moment Mary said, "Son, why have You done this to us? Your father and I have been searching for You with great sorrow."

Jesus told her, "Why did you seek Me? Didn't you know I must be about My Father's business?"

Mary and Joseph did not understand what He meant by saying such a thing.

Jesus went back to Nazareth with them and obeyed everything they told Him to do. He continued to grow and learn. Mary kept all these things in her heart.

Many years passed. One day Jesus knew it was time for Him to leave His home. He needed to go tell all who would listen how much God, their Father, loved them.

Jesus and the Children

Mark 9–10; Luke 18

A small girl and her mother stood a little apart from a group of men gathered near a village well.

"I tell you, it's true," a gray-bearded man insisted, waving his hands wildly in the still air. "It happened in Capernaum. Within the hour, word of it ran through the village like a dog after a quail!"

"What happened? What are you talking about?" a younger man demanded.

"Jesus, the son of Joseph the carpenter, has set loose tongues wagging again."

"It isn't the first time and won't be the last," someone sneered. An unpleasant laugh followed.

The little girl buried her fingers in her mother's tunic. "Why do they speak so of Jesus?" she whispered. "I thought He did good things.

"Hush, child. He does, but if the men see we are listening to them, they will send us away," her mother warned. "I want to hear more about Jesus."

So do I, the little girl thought but wisely kept the words locked behind her lips.

"Well?" a dark-eyed man challenged. "What has this Jesus done now?"

"Plenty." The man with the news paused. "He must be a diviner, for when He and His disciples came to Capernaum, He asked why they had been disputing along the way. No one would answer, but Jesus knew. I don't know how, but He did. He told the twelve, 'If anyone desires to be first, he shall be last of all and servant of all.'"

The listening child's mouth formed a little round *O*. Her mother was a servant in a wealthy man's home, but she was never first in anything.

The speaker ignored the indignant murmur that began. His eyes glistened. "That isn't all. Jesus took a little child and set him in the midst of the disciples. He took the child in His arms. Then he said for whoever caused a little one who believed in Him to stumble, it would be better for him if a millstone were hung around his neck and he were thrown into the sea!"

"With that kind of talk, soon our children will be rising up against us," someone objected. "Has He forgotten children are to honor their fathers and mothers? Or does He throw away the Law of Moses?"

"Come, daughter," the woman whispered. "We must go."

"Mother, will you take me to see Jesus?" the

child pleaded, trotting beside her mother.

"Yes, if He comes near to where we are."

"I am glad." The little girl skipped along. "I hope He will come soon."

Before long, her wish came true. Jesus came to the region of Judea by the other side of the Jordan. As usual, a great multitude of people gathered to hear His teachings. Among them were the woman and her daughter. Unfortunately, the crowd was so great they could not get near Him.

"Please, let us through," the mother pleaded. "I want Jesus to touch my child and bless her."

"Woman, be gone," some of the disciples said. "Jesus is too busy for children."

Jesus heard them and was greatly displeased. "Let the little children come to Me and forbid them not, for of such is the kingdom of God. . . . Whoever does not receive the kingdom of God as a little child will by no means enter it."

One by one, Jesus took the children up in His arms and blessed them. When it was the little girl's turn, she looked deep into the kind eyes that smiled at her. Long after she forgot the words of Jesus' blessing, she remembered the look in the Master's eyes.

Daughter
of Jairus

Matthew 9; Mark 5; Luke 8

When word about Jesus being able to heal all kinds of illnesses and afflictions spread, more and more people came to Him, begging Him to simply touch them, so they might be made well. Wherever He traveled, whether it was to cities, villages, or the smallest hamlets, great crowds of people sought Him out. Jesus made no distinction between rich and poor, mighty and weak. He loved and had compassion on all. He rewarded those who came to Him in faith, believing in His power, by making them whole. Nothing could withstand the power of God given to His Son, Jesus. Leprosy and demons fled before His touch. Even death could not prevail when Jesus passed by.

One day Jairus—one of the rulers of the synagogue—came to Jesus, where He stood by the sea. Jairus fell down in front of Jesus and worshipped Him. Then he said, "My child is dying. She is my only daughter, about twelve years of age. Please, good Master, come to my house and lay Your hands on her, that she may be healed. I know if You do this, she will live."

Jesus could not refuse such a request or such faith. He went with Jairus, and a great multitude followed and pressed around Him. Along the way, a desperate woman who had been sick for twelve years touched the hem of His garment and was instantly made whole.

"Who touched my clothes?" Jesus demanded, knowing some of His power had gone out of Him.

His disciples replied, "You see the multitude thronging around You, and yet You ask who touched You?"

The woman, who knew what had happened to her, came and fell down before Him, fearful and trembling. She confessed what she had done.

Jesus said, "Daughter, your faith has made you well. Go in peace and be healed of your affliction."

While Jesus was still speaking to the woman who had been healed, certain men came from the ruler of the synagogue's house. "Your daughter is dead," they said to Jairus. "Why trouble the Teacher any further?"

The sad news went straight to Jairus's heart. If Jesus had not tarried to talk to the woman in the crowd, He would have reached the child sooner and saved her.

Before Jairus could speak, Jesus quickly said, "Do not be afraid. Only believe."

When they reached the house, He saw a multitude of weeping people. Jesus asked, "Why are you making such a commotion? The child is not dead but sleeping."

The people laughed in scorn, but Jesus put the disbelievers out. He took the child's parents, and those who were with Him, and entered the room where the child lay. He took her hand and said, "*Talitha, cumi,*" which means, "Little girl, I say to you, arise."

The child immediately opened her eyes, got up from the bed, and walked. Jairus and his wife and all present were overcome with astonishment.

Then Jesus commanded them strictly to tell no one what had happened. He told her parents to give their daughter something to eat.

It had not mattered that Jesus was not there when those around the child pronounced her dead. Once He came and took her hand, the daughter of Jairus was restored to perfect health—and Jairus and his wife rejoiced.

A Lad Shares His Lunch

Matthew 14; Mark 6; Luke 9; John 6

From village to village, city to city, Jesus traveled. News of His coming never failed to create a stir among the people.

As the time of the Jewish Passover drew near, word reached those by the Sea of Galilee, also called the Sea of Tiberias, that Jesus was on His way.

"Jesus is going to speak on the mountainside!" people shouted. "Come. Let us hurry to see Him. Perhaps He will heal someone, as He has done in other places."

A huge crowd soon assembled and followed Jesus and His disciples. A certain young lad who was determined not to be left behind trotted after them. Unlike others who foolishly took no food with them, the boy had gathered up five small barley loaves and two small fish. Growling stomachs made it hard to listen, even to someone who was said to be a great Teacher!

As the multitude streamed after Jesus, the boy listened hard to hear what they were saying.

"Jesus heals sick people."

"He makes blind eyes see. He opens deaf ears so people can hear."

"Jesus makes lame people walk."

The lad's mouth dropped open in amazement. Did Jesus really, truly do all those wonderful things? Would He heal someone today?

It took time to climb up the side of the mountain. The lad was glad for the abundant grass beneath his bare feet. It tickled his toes. The only problem was, he couldn't see Jesus very well because of all the tall people around him.

Inch by inch, he squirmed his way through the crowd until he reached the front row. There he planted his tired feet on the ground, crossed his arms, and waited for Jesus to make a miracle.

Instead, Jesus said, "Where can we buy bread for these people to eat?"

The boy looked around him. He could hear the sound of more and more people coming up behind him. He grinned. Jesus didn't have to worry about feeding *him*. He had his lunch right there, ready to be eaten whenever he got hungry.

Philip, one of the apostles, looked worried. He told Jesus it would cost a great deal of money for everyone there to have even a bite of food.

Just then, Peter's brother, Andrew, looked straight at the lad who had brought a lunch. "This boy has five small barley loaves and two little fish," he told Jesus. "But what are they among so many?"

The little boy stared. He was awfully hungry. Did Jesus want him to give away his loaves and fishes? Andrew was right: What good would they do? Thousands of people had gathered on the hillside. The boy's stomach growled, but he held out his small supply of food. At least Jesus would have something to eat.

Jesus thanked God for the food. Then something strange happened. Something wonderful! Jesus began handing bread and fish to His disciples. They gave it to the people—five thousand men, as well as women and children. The food kept coming until everyone had all they could eat, even the small boy. And there were twelve baskets of food left over!

The little boy rubbed his eyes. "I don't understand it," he whispered. "How could He make so much out of five small loaves and two fish? I do know one thing: There isn't anyone here today who will ever forget what Jesus did with my lunch!"

Rhoda, a Very Excited Girl

Acts 12

Rhoda, a serving girl in the house of Mary, the mother of John Mark, felt so sad she didn't know what to do. Wicked King Herod had already killed John's brother, James, with a sword. When the king saw how much it pleased the Jews, he gave orders for his guards to seize Peter and throw him into prison. Even though the church offered constant prayers on Peter's behalf, their friend and leader remained locked behind prison doors. If only God would deliver him! The followers of Jesus' teachings needed Peter to lead and guide them in this time of persecution.

One night, while many of the faithful were gathered together praying, Rhoda heard someone at the gate. The sound of knocking followed.

Rhoda's heart fluttered. *Who can that be?* she wondered. *It is the middle of the night.* She knew she must see who was at the gate, but her mouth dried with fear. King Herod hated people who believed in Jesus. Perhaps he had sent his guards to arrest all in the household, because they served the One who had come to be their Messiah.

"The king is a terrible man," Rhoda whispered. She swallowed hard, stepped outside, and slowly walked to the gate. "Who is there?" she asked, trying to keep her voice from shaking. "What do you want at this hour?"

A deep voice answered—Peter's voice.

Peter? How had he escaped from prison?

Rhoda was so excited she forgot to unlock the gate. Instead, she ran inside, heart racing until she thought it would burst from her chest. "Peter is here!" she cried to those gathered together and praying for their dear friend at that very moment.

"You are crazy," the people told her. "It must be his angel."

"I am *not* crazy," Rhoda insisted. "Oh, my! I left him standing outside the gate."

A knocking began again. "Let me in!" Peter called.

When they opened the door, Peter came inside. His friends were filled with astonishment, but Peter raised his hand. "Peace," he said.

Rhoda and the others listened while he related a strange story. "I was sleeping," Peter said in his deep voice. "I was bound with two chains between two soldiers. There were guards before the door watching over the prison. Suddenly an angel of the Lord stood by me. A light shone in the prison, where it had been dark. The angel struck me on the side and said, 'Arise quickly!' The chains fell off my hands."

Rhoda wanted to cry out with joy. Instead she put one hand over her mouth to hold back her pleasure and listened to the rest of Peter's story.

"The angel told me to put on my clothes and my sandals, wrap my cloak around me, and follow him. I thought I was seeing a vision." The big fisherman paused to wipe his face. "We passed the first and second guard posts. When we reached the iron gate that leads to the city, it opened of its own accord. We went down a street, and the angel immediately departed."

Peter smiled. A look of gratitude lightened his craggy features. "When I finally realized what had happened, I knew for certain the Lord had sent His angel and delivered me from Herod. I came here."

Great was the rejoicing that God had set Peter free, but no one was happier than Rhoda— the serving maid who had been so excited she had left Peter standing at the gate!

Also available from
Barbour Publishing

THE TOP 100 WOMEN
OF THE BIBLE

by Pamela McQuade

ISBN 978-1-59789-669-6

If it's true that people learn best by
example, here are 100 examples of women
who changed the world—whether for
good or ill. In this book you'll find brief
biographies of the 100 most important
women in the Bible—from Abigail to
Zipporah—along with thought-provoking
devotional and inspirational takeaways.
Embrace the truths you discover in *The
Top 100 Women of the Bible*—and become
more, every day, the woman God wants
you to be.